shake, rattle & read!

IN THE SNOW

Written by
Madeline Tyler

Illustrated by
Amy Li

BookLife
PUBLISHING

©2019
BookLife Publishing Ltd.
King's Lynn
Norfolk, PE30 4LS

ISBN: 978-1-78637-749-4

Written by:
Madeline Tyler

Edited by:
John Wood

Illustrated by:
Amy Li

A catalogue record for this book is available from the British Library.

To find out how to read this book, turn to the back cover.

All images courtesy of Shutterstock. With thanks to Getty Images, Thinkstock Photo and iStockphoto.

Cover - KateChe, Pattern image, flovie, Toluk, Anna Timoshenko, masher. Recurring backgrounds and font - KateChe, Pattern image, malven57. Recurring brushes - Toluk (grunge), flovie (spots/snow), Anna Timoshenko (rock cracks), Grinbox (animal fur), Irina Vaneeva, ekmelica (water splashes), Igor Vitkovskiy (snow flakes). 4-7 – masher, Nadezhda Molkentin, 22-23 – oxanakot, Tartila.

Can you use your imagination to take a trip through the snow?

Follow the

INSTRUCTIONS

on each page and see what you can find.

This **polar bear** is covered in snow!

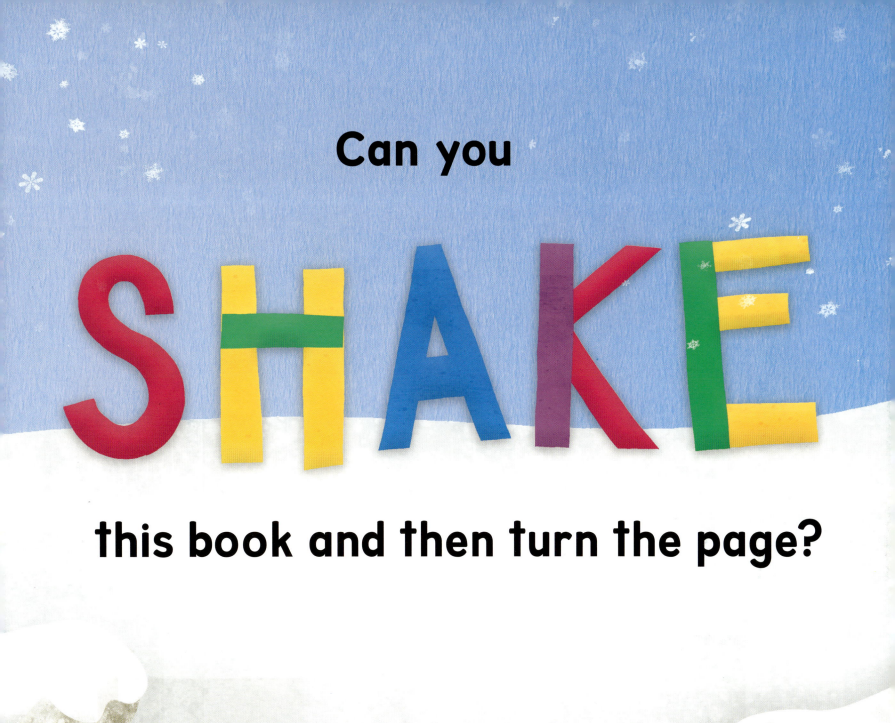

Can you

SHAKE

this book and then turn the page?

That is much better!

These penguins
are walking in a line.

POKE

the penguins gently
and then turn the page.

Oops, the penguins
have slipped on the ice!

There is an **orca** swimming in the sea.

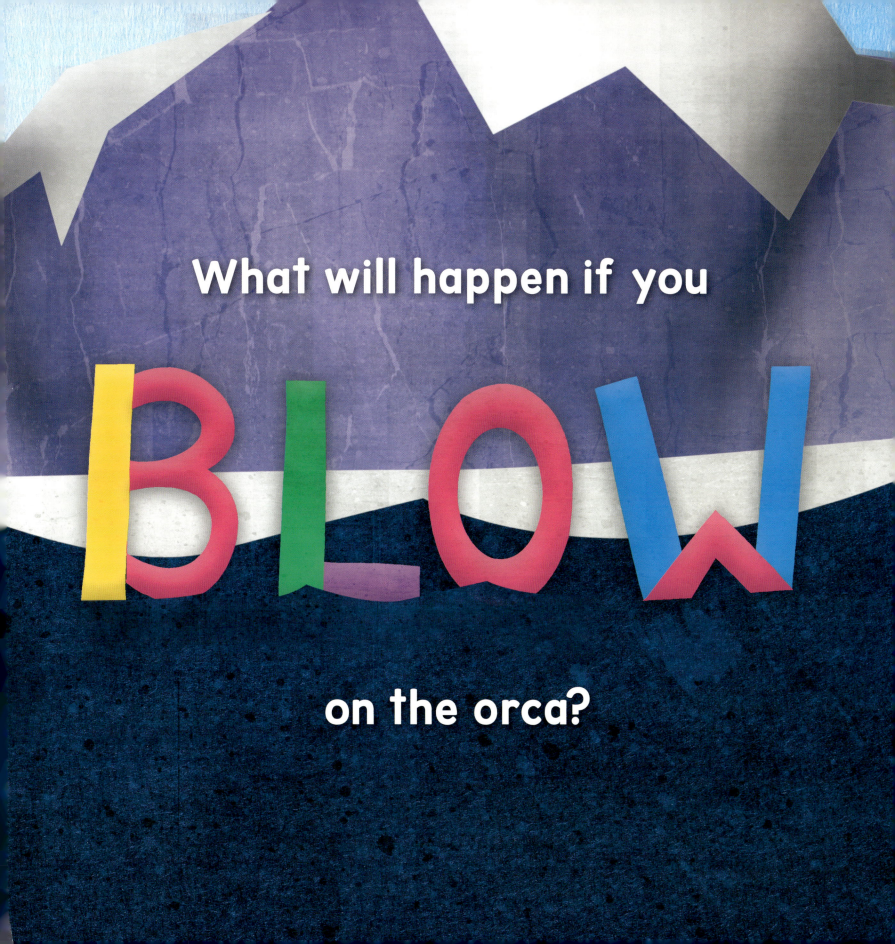

What will happen if you

BLOW

on the orca?

The orca is blowing
through its blowhole!

That is how it breathes.

There are some **seals**
on this iceberg.

Can you

this book to the left and turn the page?

That looks like fun!

Who is hiding under the water?

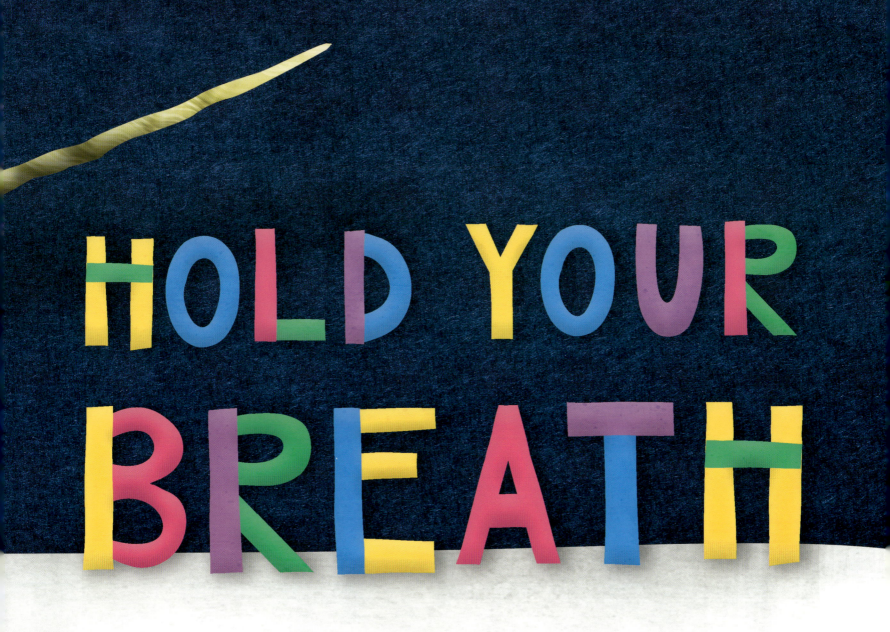

HOLD YOUR BREATH

and turn the page. Are you ready?

It is a **narwhal!**

Look at that long tooth.

Can you count all the animals in the picture?